HERE A CHICK,

by Bruce McMillan

Lothrop, Lee & Shepard Books / New York

In memory of Dad

Library of Congress Cataloging in Publication Data. McMillan, Bruce. Here a chick, there a chick. Summary: Photographs of baby chicks are used to illustrate such opposite concepts as inside/outside, asleep/awake, and alone/together. 1. English language—Synonyms and antonyms—Juvenile literature. [1. English language—Synonyms and antonyms. 2. Chickens—Pictorial works] I. Title. PE1591.M44 1983 428.1 82-20348 ISBN 0-688-02000-3 ISBN 0-688-02001-1 (lib. bdg.)

THERE A CHICK

Begin

JP
M

Inside

Outside

Here

There

Straight

Crooked

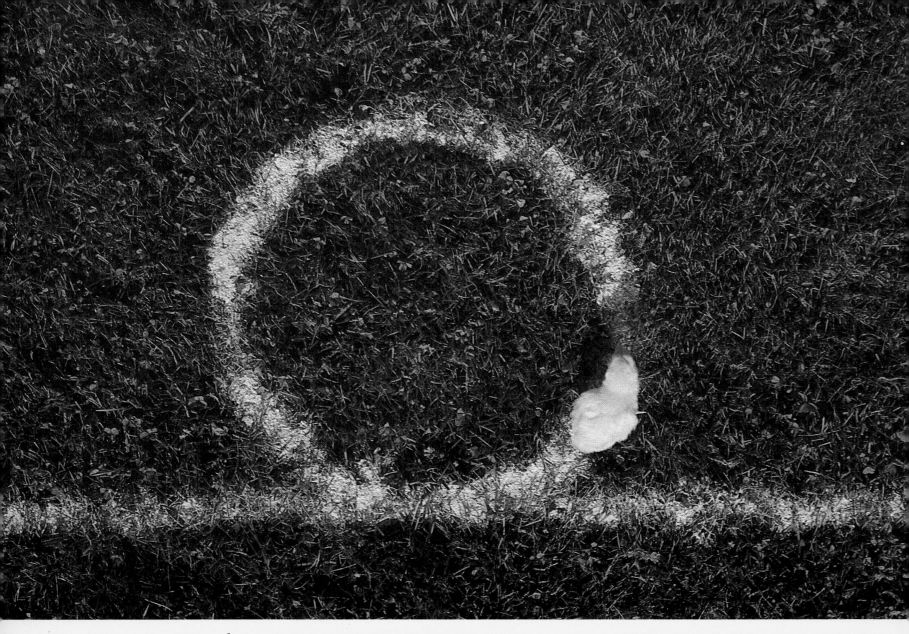

Round

and Around

Left

Right

Up

Down

Stand

Sit

Asleep

Awake

In

Out

High

Low

Alone

Together

End

ABOUT THIS BOOK:

Several people helped make this book possible. I wish to thank Alex Roubo and the CoHen Hatchery, Inc., for providing the chicks, Mike and Sharie Hodge for the use of their lush green lawn, and professional chick handlers and trainers Brett and Terry McMillan. I could not have done this book without their help and cooperation.

The baby chicks are the DeKalb-Warren breed, a sex-link cross. The chicks in the photographs are all males, because only male chicks of this breed are full yellow. We kept some females from the same hatching, however, to raise as laying hens.

This book was photographed using a Nikon F2 camera with the following Nikkor lenses: 28mm, 55mm Micro, 105mm, and 200mm; either no filter, an 82A, or an 82B, depending on the light temperature; sunlight with a reflector; and Ektachrome 200 film, processed by Meisel Photochrome.

ABOUT THE AUTHOR:

Bruce McMillan grew up in Maine, earned a B.S. degree in biology from the University of Maine in Orono, and worked briefly as a public television producer/director and as an island caretaker, before settling into a career as a photographer and writer. He is the photographer and author of seven children's books and two for adults. Mr. McMillan makes his home in Shapleigh, Maine, with his wife, Terry, and son, Brett.